The
Talyllyn
Railway
in Colour

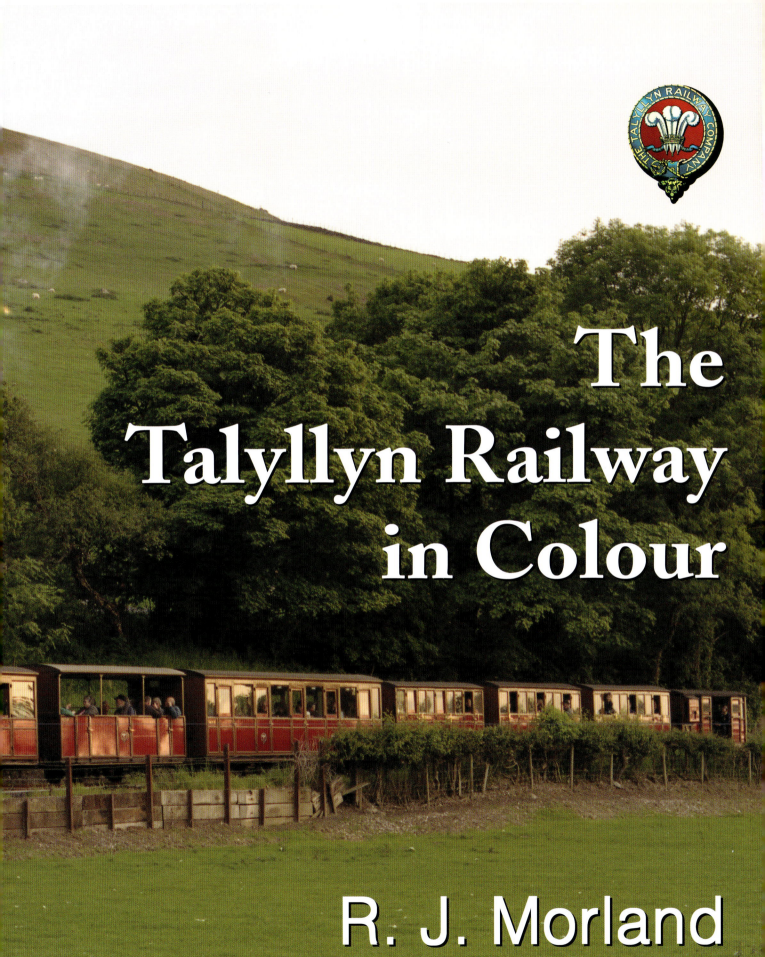

The
Talyllyn Railway
in Colour

R. J. Morland

First edition published in Great Britain in 2005 by R. J. Morland

1, Mortlock Close, Melbourn, Royston, Hertfordshire, SG8 6DA.
robert.morland@virgin.net

Graham Thomas filling No 1's tank at Dolgoch.

August 1997

Text and photographs copyright © R. J. Morland.
Map of the Talyllyn Railway copyright © J. Milner.
Talyllyn Railway crest reproduced with permission of the Talyllyn Railway Company.
The moral right of R. J. Morland to be identified as the author of this work has been asserted.

A CIP catalogue record for this book is available from The British Library.

ISBN 0-9549893-0-9   ISBN-13 978-0-9549893-0-9

Designed by R. J. Morland.
Typeset in Adobe HelvLight and Adobe Caslon.
Colour photography by R. J. Morland and G. R. Morland.
Printed in Wales by HSW Print, Tonypandy, Rhondda, CF40 2XX.

Photographs taken using a Bronica SQ medium format camera and Fuji NPS and NPH 120 roll film.

Proceeds from the sale of this book are being donated to help with the maintenance and development of the Talyllyn Railway.

Previous pages: Locomotive No 2 'Dolgoch' with an up evening special train running through the loop at Brynglas, fired by Alex Eyres.

May 2003

Front page: Ken Timpson lighting up locomotive No 1 'Talyllyn' in Pendre shed.

July 1990

Contents

Notes for the Reader

Talyllyn Locomotive names and numbers:

No 1 'Talyllyn'	No 6 'Douglas'
No 2 'Dolgoch'	No 7 'Tom Rolt'
No 3 'Sir Haydn'	No 8 'Merseysider'
No 4 'Edward Thomas'	No 9 'Alf'
No 5 'Midlander'	No 10 'Bryneglwys'

Train directions:

On the Talyllyn, 'up' trains travel up the valley from Tywyn Wharf to Nant Gwernol and 'down' trains travel down the valley from Nant Gwernol to Tywyn Wharf.

No 7 arrives at Rhydyronen with an up train, driven by Maurice Wilson.

September 1991

Talyllyn Lake looking westwards from Bwlch Llyn Bach. Cader Idris is off to the right of the picture. The Talyllyn Railway starts its journey in the valley beyond the lake and runs away from the camera down towards the coast of Cardigan Bay.

September 2003

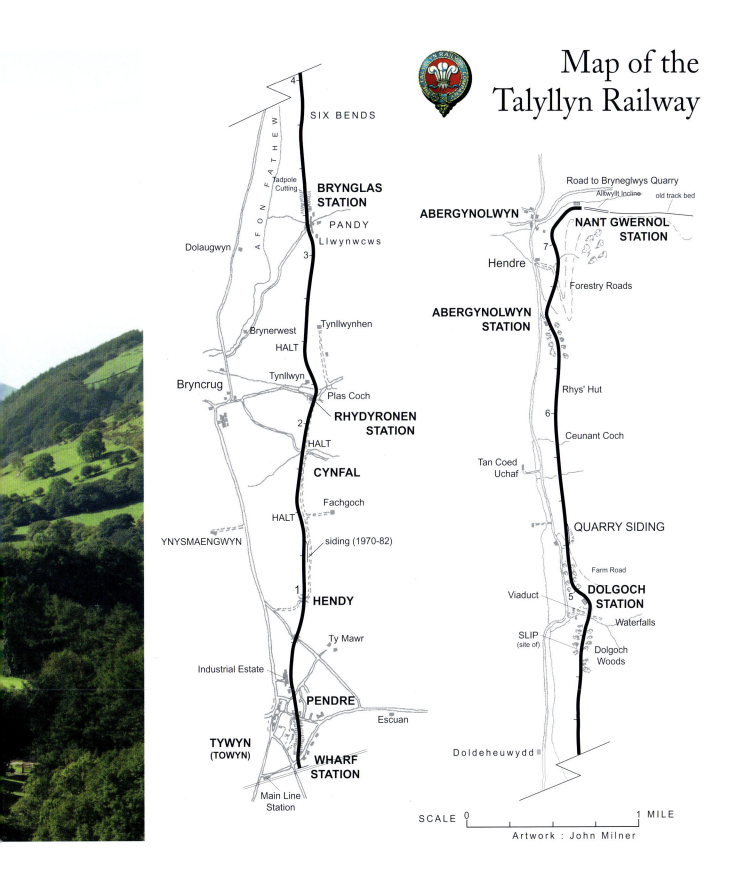

Map of the Talyllyn Railway

SIX BENDS

AFON FATHEW

Tadpole Cutting

4

BRYNGLAS STATION

PANDY

Llwynwcws

3

Dolaugwyn

Tynllwynhen

Brynerwest
HALT

Bryncrug

Tynllwyn

Plas Coch

RHYDYRONEN STATION

2

HALT

CYNFAL

Fachgoch

HALT

siding (1970-82)

YNYSMAENGWYN

1

HENDY

Ty Mawr

Industrial Estate

PENDRE

Escuan

TYWYN (TOWYN)

WHARF STATION

Main Line Station

Road to Bryneglwys Quarry

Alltwyllt Incline   old track bed

ABERGYNOLWYN

NANT GWERNOL STATION

Hendre

7

Forestry Roads

ABERGYNOLWYN STATION

Rhys' Hut

6

Ceunant Coch

Tan Coed Uchaf

QUARRY SIDING

Farm Road

Viaduct   **DOLGOCH STATION**
5

Waterfalls

SLIP
(site of)   Dolgoch Woods

Doldeheuwydd

SCALE   0   1 MILE

Artwork : John Milner

Foreword

Most of us are familiar with the "public" face of our chosen heritage railway. Not all photographers are lucky enough to have the privileged position of being able to go behind the scenes at, as it were, the drop of a lens-cap. Bob Morland, as a member of the Talyllyn's Locomotive Department over many years, has made the most of his opportunities, and in this book gives us as intimate (in the best possible sense) a picture of the Talyllyn Railway as could possibly be achieved.

It is a celebration in pictures of what the TR means to him, and he has managed to capture, I think, what it means to most of us. His photographs are affectionate, informative, entertaining and, above all, a genuine expression of the Talyllyn as it really is. Any railway is an entity in itself - Bob catches that - but it is the people who make it tick that matter, and a wide range of them appears here, doing what they love doing best and in essence "being" the Talyllyn.

I took my first Talyllyn photograph - snapshot would really be a more accurate description of it - in 1954, but very few that I have taken in more than 50 years since match up to Bob's. One of my pleasures (and only one of many) in looking at the pictures in this book has been the way that the less visual aspects of the railway have not been ignored; a pile of fish plates for instance, a diesel buffer beam or still hot firebox-ash being disposed of. All these images help to make up an overview of a living railway, and that is the way it should be, for the TR is nothing if not a living railway.

The Talyllyn is a family railway too, and this also Bob has succeeded in drawing out - if you doubt me, take a quick look at pages 206 and 218. The names of the many volunteers portrayed here span family decades too - fathers, sons, daughters and many more.

'The Talyllyn Railway in Colour' is a labour of love and anyone who sees its pictures will love the labour that has gone into producing it. I treasure my copy and wish it every possible success.

Christopher Awdry

Driver David Ratcliff and fireman Keith Foster survey the road ahead from No 2, waiting to depart from Rhydyronen.

September 2001

Introduction

The Talyllyn Railway has been a part of my life since 1970 when, at the age of fifteen, I started working as a volunteer in the Traffic Department. Since then I have grown to love this most special railway, and the people who run it together.

The Talyllyn really is a part of the family for those of us who spend our free time, often a long way from home, helping to preserve and operate the railway for pleasure. We grow up, and grow old, with the community of characters who make the Talyllyn so special. People meet up, get together and before long the next generation of volunteers comes along to continue the tradition. We are all privileged to be a part of the life of the Talyllyn, and this book is a celebration of all that is best about it.

The photographs which follow are a selection that, for me, say the most about the railway, its unique locomotives and rolling stock, its countryside and its people. I hope that you enjoy looking through them as much as I have enjoyed waiting for the trains – and the sun – to capture the images for you.

Bob Morland

Bob Morland

Acknowledgements

I am grateful for the help and assistance of many friends on the Talyllyn Railway in putting this book together. I am in particular indebted to the working volunteers and staff on the Talyllyn who have tolerated my presence taking photographs of them in all kinds of unusual places on and around our railway over many years.

I would like to thank John Bate, who has kindly proof-read the text, John Smallwood, who has helped with the significant task of checking the captions and Christopher Awdry, for writing the Foreword. Thanks are also due to John Milner for granting permission for use of his excellent plan of the line, which first appeared in John Bate's book, 'The Chronicles of Pendre Sidings', published by Rail Romances, from which I have also referred for certain facts used in the captions. Other details have been obtained from the book 'Talyllyn Railway Locomotives and Rolling Stock', written by John Bate, David Mitchell and Nigel Adams and published by Cheona Publications.

Producing this book has been immensely enjoyable, but would not have been possible without the assistance of Karl Hewson, whose advice on DTP and colour management has been invaluable.

Lastly, I would like to thank my wife Gill for her assistance with the difficult job of selecting photographs for the book, her tireless support with quality control and her great forbearance throughout the entire production process.

Dedication

This book is dedicated to the staff and volunteers of the Talyllyn Railway, without whom there would be no railway to photograph, and no trains for us all to travel on.

Looking north east up the Afon Dysynni valley, just to the north of the Fathew valley up which the Talyllyn Railway runs. This valley is dominated on the right hand side by Bird Rock (Craig Yr Aderyn), so named because it is the unusual inland home to a colony of Cormorants.

June 1993

A view of the sunset over Cardigan Bay from the promenade at Tywyn

August 2000

Tywyn Wharf

Original Talyllyn locomotive No 2 'Dolgoch' leaves the old station at Tywyn Wharf with an up train, driven by David Ratcliff. No 2 was built by Fletcher Jennings and Co at their Lowca Works in Whitehaven and delivered new to the railway in 1866. Apart from occasional trips away for repairs and to star in special events, No 2 has spent its entire life on the Talyllyn. It was the only operational locomotive when the line was taken over by the Talyllyn Railway Preservation Society in 1951. Although in very poor mechanical condition, No 2 gallantly ran the train service alone throughout 1951. Without No 2 there would probably be no Talyllyn Railway for us all to enjoy today.

September 1991

Tywyn Wharf

Most visitors will start their Talyllyn journey at Wharf Station, but it wasn't always this way. Originally named Kings, this station was built for the railway's opening in 1865, primarily to allow trans-shipment of slate, conveyed by the Talyllyn from the Bryneglwys Slate Quarries, on to the newly-opened Cambrian Coast main line.

Passenger trains commenced their journeys at Pendre, which was considered closer to the town centre at the time. Only much later, when tourism began to develop, did Wharf become a passenger station. In pre-society days there was

no run-round loop here, so passenger trains had to be propelled from Pendre to commence their journey at Wharf.

The old station building from 1865 survives at Wharf, although it has been extended and altered several times. The most significant development here in the line's history has been the recent completion of the new building, housing a much enlarged museum and café, together with improved offices and staff accommodation.

No 4 whistles for departure with a morning train from the new Wharf station, which opened in 2005. The original station remains in the foreground while behind is the new building, housing an enlarged museum, café and offices for the railway.

March 2005

The new Wharf station building under construction, viewed from the west side of the main line railway.

August 2004

A view of the new Wharf building from the station approach during construction. The roof is on and the contractors are working to complete the structure before fitting-out commences.

August 2004

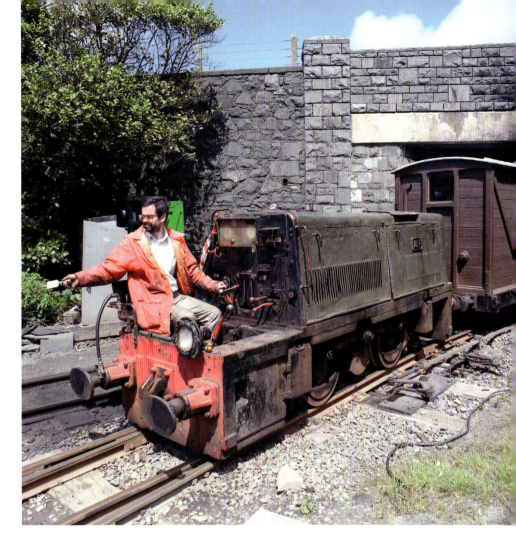

Andy Best driving diesel No 9 'Alf' arriving at Wharf with an engineering train. In his right hand is the single line token for the section between Wharf and Pendre. No 9 was originally built for the National Coal Board for underground use at the Huncoat Colliery in Lancashire, which fortuitously used the Talyllyn's unusual track gauge of 2' 3". No 9 and an identical unit were inspected at a Manchester scrap yard in 1970. They were both purchased and No 9 first worked on the Talyllyn in August 1971. The name 'Alf' was originally a joke about No 9's origins - Lord Alf Robens was Chairman of the Coal Board at the time.

May 2002

Diesel No 9's name plate

June 2004

Traffic Manager David Leech using the Wharf Electric Key Token (EKT) machine in a temporary housing, provided whilst the Traffic Office was being reconstructed. This was part of the extensive new building work at Wharf which took place between 2002 and 2005.

May 2002

No 4, 'Edward Thomas', running as 'Peter Sam', leaving Wharf driven by Martin Lester. No 4 was built by Kerr Stuart of Stoke on Trent and delivered new to the neighbouring Corris Railway in 1921. After the Corris closed in 1948, No 4, together with No 3, was stored at Machynlleth until both were purchased for the Talyllyn in 1951. The engine was named 'Edward Thomas' after the manager of the railway in 1950 when the Preservation Society took over.

June 1993

Malcolm Brown eases No 2 over the points at Wharf as he runs the locomotive round its train. The engine will reverse back over the line in the foreground to take coal and water before taking up its position at the front of the train for the next journey up the line.

August 1989

Four generations of Talyllyn electrical engineers came together to work on rewiring the power, signalling and telephone systems at Wharf during the rebuilding project. From left to right are Andy Best, Ian Dods, Nick Smith and Don Southgate. Their work on the railway spans more than five decades.

May 2002

Keith Foster on No 2 preparing to propel an Empty Coaching Stock (ECS) train back to Pendre at the end of the day. In front of the locomotive is original Talyllyn Brake and Luggage Van No 5, built by Brown Marshalls of Birmingham and delivered new to the railway in 1865.

September 2001

No 1 'Talyllyn' and vintage train at Wharf for an evening photo shoot. Guard Walter Crowe is studying his watch whilst driver Paul Shuttleworth and fireman Alex Eyres look on. No 1 was the first locomotive to run on the Talyllyn. It was built by Fletcher Jennings and Co in Whitehaven and was delivered in 1864, where it helped with the construction of the line. No 1 was originally an 0-4-0 but was soon rebuilt as an 0-4-2. This was as a result of much 'vertical oscillation' of the original design, due to the long overhang behind the driving wheels. Like No 2, 'Talyllyn' has spent its entire working life on the railway whose name it bears.

July 2001

Valves controlling steam to injectors and blower on top of No 2's boiler

March 2005

Four of the Talyllyn's six steam locomotives are pictured here during a night photo shoot with floodlights. From left to right are No 6, No 1, No 3 and No 7.

September 1995

No 3 'Sir Haydn' leaving Wharf driven by Mike Davies. No 3 was one of two Corris engines purchased by the Talyllyn in 1951. Built by the Hughes Engine Company of Loughborough in 1878 its initial trials on the Talyllyn were unsuccessful due to its narrow tyres and the poor state of the Talyllyn track when the Society took over in 1951. After a number of derailments it was put into store for two years and finally entered service in 1953. The locomotive was named 'Sir Haydn' after Sir Henry Haydn Jones, owner of the railway until 1950.

September 1994

Andy Statham oiling the plain axleboxes of the Talyllyn Goods Van. The body of this van was used as a shed at Rhydyronen for many years but has now been fully restored and is used for special trains. On this occasion it was forming part of a goods train during the weekend of the Annual General Meeting of the Talyllyn Railway Preservation Society.

September 2000

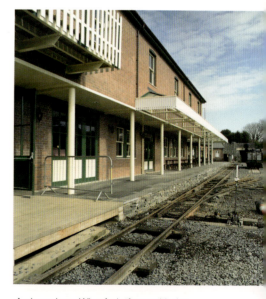

A view along Wharf platform with the new building on the left. The Narrow Gauge Museum is nearest to the camera with the café beyond.

March 2005

Winston McCanna filling in the blackboard advertising 'Chris Awdry Day' featuring 'Duncan' (alias No 6 'Douglas') and 'Sir Handel' (alias No 3 'Sir Haydn'). The Talyllyn runs special days for children featuring the railway's engines which were written into the Revd Awdry's popular books.

May 2002

No 2's air brake hose, connected to the train. The black handle isolates the engine air supply from the train pipe.

March 2005

No 2 waiting to depart from Wharf with the 02:10 train for Nant Gwernol during one of the Talyllyn's popular all-night steamings. Driver Pete Mintoft looks into the cab whilst staff and intrepid passengers chat on the platform.

July 2001

WHARF TO PENDRE

No 2, driven by Graham Thomas, hauls its train up Wharf cutting at the start of its journey to Nant Gwernol.

March 2005

Wharf to Pendre

On leaving Wharf, the train passes immediately under the Brynhyfryd Road bridge and into a deep tree-lined cutting. The gradient here used to be a harsh start to the journey, made worse in damp conditions by the overhanging trees that dropped their leaves onto the rails. In 1979 the railway dug out the cutting to ease the maximum grade at this point from a challenging 1 in 60 to a more reasonable 1 in 150, making the initial climb out of Wharf much easier for the locomotives.

On the north side of the line there used to be a siding into which loaded slate wagons were pushed. These were then hand shunted to descend by gravity under the Brynhyfryd bridge to be sorted into one of the fan of sidings that once occupied the Wharf site.

Passing under the Llys Cadfan footbridge and then School Bridge the line levels out and emerges into the yard at Pendre.

No 6 'Duncan' ('Douglas') with an up train in Wharf cutting, driven by Ray Reid. No 6 was built in 1918 by Andrew Barclay of Kilmarnock for service with the Admiralty Air Service Construction Corps. It worked at various RAF sites until 1945 when it was put into storage and subsequently purchased by Abelson (Engineers) Ltd of Birmingham. It was donated to the Talyllyn and named 'Douglas' after Douglas Abelson, Managing Director of the Abelson company. It entered service on the Talyllyn in 1954.

June 2004

Two ground disc signals, located close to the Brynhyfryd Road bridge, control the entry to Wharf station. The signal on the left shows when the points are set for the yard. The one on the right is 'off' in this shot, indicating that the points are set for the platform.

June 2004

Close to the first quarter mile post in Wharf cutting are connection boxes for signal and telephone equipment.

June 2004

The Wharf home signal protects the station. The panel above the colour lights displays a 'U' when the station is unmanned. The panel below displays two white lights as a 'calling on' signal for moves other than to an empty platform road.

March 2005

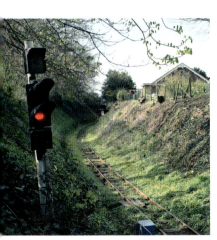

In Spring the Wharf cutting is a carpet of celandines.

March 2005

Driver John Scott relaxes on No 1 at the end of the day whilst the fireman, Peter Fuller, propels the empty train back under the Llys Cadfan footbridge to Pendre.

June 1994

The crew of No 3 waiting under School Bridge for the guard to set the road so they can propel their train into the carriage shed at Pendre.

June 1995

Fireman John Burton keeps a good lookout ahead as No 3 propels its train up Wharf cutting in the late afternoon sunshine.

June 1995

TYWYN PENDRE

A busy scene in the yard at Pendre. Dave Jacques on No 4 waits to come off shed to pick up its train whilst No 7 'Tom Rolt', driven by Phil Guest, passes with a train for Nant Gwernol. No 7 was built at Pendre from parts of a locomotive supplied in 1948 by Andrew Barclay to the Bord na Mona in Ireland. Originally designed to burn peat as fuel it was not successful and was stored out of use until purchased by the Talyllyn in 1969. A new design was created by Talyllyn Chief Engineer John Bate to use the main components and No 7 was completed in 1991. The locomotive is named after one of the founders of the Talyllyn Railway Preservation Society.

July 1992

Driver Roy Smith on No 7 eases the stock out of the West Carriage Shed in the morning, ready for the day's work.
June 1993

Tywyn Pendre

Pendre is the engineering hub of the Talyllyn Railway. The original Works and Locomotive Shed remain from the 1860s, but new buildings have been added to accommodate the enlarged needs of the railway as it has grown under Preservation Society management. In particular, two large carriage sheds have been built, enabling all the railway's rolling stock to be stabled under cover – an important requirement given the nature of the Welsh weather and the historical importance of the Talyllyn's original vehicles.

Carriage Sheds

The first carriage shed reached on the journey from Wharf is the West Shed, on which building work for the first phase started in 1970. It was constructed in three phases and completed in 1984. The eastern end of this shed also accommodates the Paint Shop, which can be isolated from the rest of the shed by doors to keep the environment warm and dust-free for painting work. Here also is the blockpost where the driver, or a blockman if Pendre is manned, will exchange Electric Key Tokens for permission to proceed into the next single line section to Brynglas.

An afternoon shot of driver Martin Lester and fireman John Burton shunting with No 3 at the west end of Pendre.

June 1993

No 7 has just pushed its train into the West Carriage Shed at the end of the day and driver Phil Guest is preparing to uncouple the locomotive.

July 1992

Having just withdrawn its train from the West Carriage Shed, No 6, driven by Terry Gurd, sets back onto the main line at Pendre. The train will pause for the guard to do a brake test before it proceeds to Wharf to pick up passengers for its first trip of the day.

June 2003

Blockman David Lowe exchanges single line tokens with David Jones driving No 4 as it passes Pendre Blockpost with an up train. The driver is giving up the token for the section from Wharf and receiving the next token, which allows him to travel as far as Brynglas.

July 1992

Assistant Katie Willers brushing out a carriage in the West Shed prior to the train service whilst guard Lawrence Garvey polishes the windows. Every Talyllyn train is thoroughly cleaned each morning by the dedicated crew.

August 2003

Guard Roger Whitehouse oils an axlebox on original Talyllyn carriage No 4, affectionately known from early preservation days as 'Limping Lulu'. This was on account of her pronounced lean to one side, since rectified. Now just known as 'Lulu', this unique carriage was built by the Lancaster Wagon Works and delivered to the Talyllyn in 1866. The Talyllyn is privileged to have in regular use both its original locomotives and all its original passenger rolling stock from the 1860s. The old carriages have plain bearings which require regular lubrication. This calls for some dexterity on the part of the guard.

June 2003

Rob Plumridge cleaning the windows of carriage No 18. The only one of its type, this carriage was built as a volunteer project and completed in 1965. It is one of only two Talyllyn bogie coaches with brass grab handles on the platform side, the other being No 16.

June 2004

Guard Roger Whitehouse polishing the brass door handles of carriage No 22. One of a series of 'standard' Talyllyn carriages, No 22 entered service in 1972.

June 2003

Roy Smith driving No 7 with an Empty Coaching Stock (ECS) train to Wharf.

June 1993

John Smallwood cleaning the front end of one of the Talyllyn saloon carriages. Usually marshalled at the front of the train, the saloons collect dirt from the steam engines that are coupled to them, and require regular cleaning so that passengers can enjoy the sight of the locomotive and crew, working to pull the train up the line. The Talyllyn's carriages are maintained by a dedicated team of volunteers known as the 'Bodgers'. Their work ranges from paintwork and varnishing through minor repairs to complete rebuilding of carriages.

August 2003

Graham Jenkins on diesel No 9 shunting a Talyllyn slate wagon and open carriage No 12 at the west end of Pendre yard. Carriage No 12 entered service on the Talyllyn in 1956.

June 1993

A shot of the front end and radiator of diesel No 9 in the yard at Pendre. The radiator grille makes a convenient storage place for coupling hooks, used for engineering trains, and on this occasion also a decorative plastic flower.

June 2004

At the end of the West Carriage Shed is the Paint Shop, which is known to gather all sorts of equipment and tools, some of which are only loosely connected with painting. The yellow and red dome-topped cabinets are spare Electric Key Token instruments.

June 2004

Fireman Mike Parrott enjoys the afternoon sun as No 2 coasts past Pendre Blockpost. Blockman David Lowe is preparing to exchange tokens with the driver.

July 1992

Pendre Yard

The loop at Pendre is used for crossing trains in some timetables, and also leads to the North Carriage Shed. This was built in 1959, partly on the site of an old hay barn, which features in some photographs taken in the early 1950s and before. Locomotive No 1 'Talyllyn' was placed in this barn with a life-expired boiler in 1952. Behind and alongside the North Shed are the Carpentry Shop, Electrician's Shop and Stores.

Driver Terry Gurd on No 6 pauses outside Pendre blockpost before departing for Wharf with an ECS train.

June 2003

Driver Graham Thomas on No 1 hauls the Talyllyn Vintage Train out of the North Carriage Shed ready for the day's work.

August 1997

Graham Thomas on No 1 at the west end of the Pendre loop. He is taking the engine into the North Shed, behind the photographer, to pick up its train.

August 1997

John Burton firing No 1 as it passes through Pendre yard with a train for Wharf. On the headshunt is No 3, which has finished its duties for the day and awaits its turn to enter the shed so that it is in the correct order for lighting-up in the morning.

June 1995

Robert Frost shunting with No 6 alongside the North Carriage Shed at Pendre.

May 2004

A cheerful group on the steps of Pendre Blockpost. Lawrence Garvey, Jane Garvey and Kathy Whitehouse obligingly pose for the photographer.

July 2001

On a pleasant evening, volunteers await the arrival back at Pendre of No 4, which was on a running-in turn up the line following a major overhaul. Blockman Bill Heynes signals the train whilst Alex Eyres and Pete Mintoft wait with cameras ready to capture the event.

May 2004

Driver Roy Smith on No 1 writes the numbers of the carriages forming his train in his notebook, prior to taking them to Wharf to pick up passengers. Blockman Malcolm Bryce encourages the train to depart with a green flag.

July 1990

David Jones on the footplate of No 4 in the yard at Pendre. The engine has just returned from a running-in trip up the line after a major overhaul.

May 2004

Detail of No 4's left hand side piston rod, crosshead and front driving wheel.

May 2004

In 1998 No 6 was turned to face down the valley - Talyllyn engines usually face up the valley, towards Abergynolwyn. This provided added interest for the crews and some unusual photo opportunities. Here Andy Young is firing No 6 as it hauls an up train through the yard at Pendre. The cable on No 6's rear lamp bracket is an extension lead allowing the Train Communication System to be connected when the locomotive is running the wrong way round.

June 1998

Roy Smith starts No 1, withdrawing its train from the North Carriage Shed ready to begin its day's service.

July 1990

Detail of the fireman's side injector clack valve on the side of No 2's boiler.

May 2004

Andy Young runs No 2 round its train at Pendre. Whilst the new building was being constructed at Wharf all locomotive servicing was carried out at Pendre. Lack of a loop at Wharf meant that engines ran round their trains at Pendre, which were then propelled down to pick up their passengers shortly before departure time.

September 2004

The Talyllyn's flail mower in the yard at Pendre. Designed by John Bate, this powerful machine makes short work of keeping the cuttings and hedgerows clear during the summer months. It was built at Pendre using a McConnel power arm and commenced trials in the Winter of 1998/9, entering full service later in 1999.

June 2003

Steve Griffiths checks the tightness of bolts securing the flail blades before the mower goes up the line to work. The Talyllyn doesn't commence cutting hedges and banks until June to allow time for spring flowers to bloom and birds to nest and rear young prior to disturbance of the lineside habitat. Regular mowing using the flail has kept heather and brambles in check and allowed flowers to thrive along the cuttings and embankments of the railway.

June 2003

The front end of Diesel No 10, unofficially named 'Deg' (Welsh for ten) and officially 'Bryneglwys' in the yard at Pendre. This locomotive is powered by a 100hp Dorman air-cooled engine and is capable, in an emergency, of hauling a passenger train at the Talyllyn's maximum line speed of 15 mph.

June 2004

Dave Scotson driving diesel No 8 'Merseysider' shunts stock in the yard at Pendre. In the background David Ratcliff on No 2 prepares to pull stock out of the North Carriage Shed and is in conversation with the guard, Tony Thorpe. No 8 was purchased along with two other redundant locomotives in 1969 at a scrap price of £11 per ton. They had seen use at Park Gate Steelworks. No 8 was built by Ruston & Hornsby and commenced work on the Talyllyn in 1970. It was named 'Merseysider' at the request of the Society member who funded the purchase. Recently No 8 has been extensively rebuilt with new cab and bodywork, returning to traffic in 2002.

September 1991

Driver Maurice Wilson on No 1 with a down train running through the yard at Pendre. The guard, John Newman, watches from Van No 5.

June 1994

Permanent way signs stacked outside the store at Pendre. 'C' and 'T' boards denote 'Commencement' and 'Termination' of a temporary 5mph speed restriction on the Talyllyn. The 'man struggling with umbrella' signs indicate work on the track requiring trains to sound their whistle and proceed with caution.

June 2004

Fishplates and a wheelstop stored outside the North Carriage Shed. In years gone by the Talyllyn used second-hand rail from a variety of places, and a range of different sections. Each type of rail required its own special fishplates. The railway now uses one standard section of rail so the variety of fishplates is being reduced, but a stock of various types remains.

June 2004

Malcolm Brown on No 2 shunting stock in the loop at Pendre.

August 1989

Phil Guest on No 7 runs through the yard at Pendre with a down train. Mike Parrott and Roy Milburn watch from No 2, which is sitting on the back road.

July 1992

Mike Parrott driving No 2 shunts the Vintage Train in the loop at Pendre.

August 1992

One of two displacement lubricators on the front running plate of No 2. Originally used for cylinder lubrication this function is now carried out by mechanical lubricators on all the Talyllyn engines, so No 2's old lubricators are just for decoration. They are still carefully polished by the crew every day before the locomotive leaves the shed.

May 2004

The driver's side injector outflow pipe on No 2.

March 2005

Tim Wilkinson driving the motor trolley 'Toby' through the yard at Pendre. Originally designed by John Bate and delivered to the railway in 1954, the trolley was powered by a pre-war Austin 7 engine. The engine was replaced in 1965 and again in 2001, the latest unit being a Ford diesel. The trolley is regularly used when one or two people need to move around the railway efficiently with a few tools, typically for inspection and light maintenance work.

August 2002

Detail of the controls on the motor trolley resting at Pendre.

June 2004

No 2's firebox door catches the late morning sun.

March 2005

Chris Parrott on No 2 looks down the yard to check whether the road is clear
for the engine to move off and pick up its evening train.

July 2001

Guard Nigel Adams releasing air from the connecting pipe at the east end of his train to test the operation of the air brakes. A full brake test is carried out every morning and brake continuity tests are done each time a locomotive is coupled to the train throughout the day.

July 2001

Ian Dods shunting with No 8 in the loop at Pendre.

June 1993

The railway's A.F. Trencher, used for digging trenches alongside the line to bury cables. Buried cables are much less susceptible to damage than overhead wires. Virtually all the Talyllyn's cabling is now underground due to the work of this small but effective machine, together with some hard manual digging in areas where the trencher cannot be used.

June 2004

Close-up shot of the driver's controls of the Matisa tamping machine. This is one of two units acquired in 1989, the second being used for spares. The tamper is used to consolidate ballast following track relaying, saving much manual work.

May 2004

Andrew Thomas driving No 6 light engine through the yard at Pendre. In the foreground are spare wheelsets between a wagon and the rail-mounted hydraulic press, used for pressing wheelsets and other components together when a secure and immovable fit is required.

June 2004

No 6's displacement regulator lubricator. This is filled with cylinder oil each morning and it then feeds a small amount of oil continuously into the regulator valve, housed in the casting underneath. As oil is fed it is displaced by water, which is drained out the following morning when the lubricator is refilled. A simple but effective design.

June 2004

MRFS renumbering Talyllyn wagon No 1 outside the South Shed at Pendre.
This was in preparation for a visit by the wagon to the Corris Railway.

May 2003

Liz Green on the footplate of No 6, which is wearing Air Ministry markings in honour of its origins in the Admiralty Air Service Construction Corps.

August 1996

No 6 rests in the sunshine outside the old South Carriage Shed.

September 1991

A view eastwards through Pendre yard. No 3 has just paused in the station platform with a down train. In the centre is the Locomotive Shed and to the right is the South Carriage Shed, now usually used to store out-of-service locomotives. On this occasion No 1 is just visible inside. The line to the right passes behind the shed to the works beyond.

August 1992

Locomotive Shed

The Locomotive Shed, originally built in 1866 to accommodate the railway's only two locomotives, was extended in 1968 to double its size by occupying the railway's cottage that backed onto it. The shed now has space for all the four locomotives needed by the railway's peak summer service. When a fifth engine is required, this is stabled in the old South Carriage Shed, and is hauled out to be lit up – not the best turn for the crew when the weather is wet.

Driver David Ratcliff oiling No 7 just before the locomotive is due to move off shed to commence its duties for the day.

July 1992

Jon Mann inspecting No 1's motion in the shed at the start of the day. Every locomotive has a careful visual examination each day it is in use.

August 2003

Driver John Scott polishing No 6's brass regulator lubricator during the morning preparation routine. When a cleaner is not rostered the driver and fireman work together to clean, prepare and inspect the engine for its day's work.

June 1999

Dave Jacques removing ash and clinker from No 1's firebox before lighting up. On the Talyllyn, it is usual to leave a small amount of fire in at night so that the firebox and boiler cool down slowly, reducing stress.

August 2003

Phil Mason and Nicky Fox share a joke in front of No 2 during the morning cleaning routine. Pendre is a great place to make friends and the Talyllyn has men and women in all its locomotive and traffic operating grades, including cleaners, firemen, guards, blockmen and drivers.

August 2003

Jon Mann and Andy Young in conversation outside the shed while Cattherina Hancock looks on. The hose is supplying water to No 6's well tank. 'Duncan' appears to be studying the traffic cone, which is placed at the end of the shed once engines move out as a reminder to people of the exposed inspection pit.

August 2003

Helen Carlyle cleaning the top of No 2's boiler in the shed. On the Talyllyn, paintwork is first wiped down to remove dirt and then a small amount of oil is applied on a rag and rubbed in to provide a gloss finish.
August 2003

Katie Willers cleaning the paintwork on No 1's driver's side bunker.

August 2003

Fireman Ken Timpson lighting up No 1. The Talyllyn light-up routine starts with the fireman cleaning the smokebox and grate. The fire is lit with a few rags soaked in diesel oil. A strong fire is then built with wood before coal is added. The secret is to build the fire gradually, adding fuel as it burns away. This keeps the fire bright, reduces smoke and makes steam quickly.

July 1990

No 4's fire is burning well shortly after light-up. Talyllyn engines are lit up a little over three hours before they are due to depart from Wharf with their first train. The pressure gauge usually moves off its mark within an hour and the locomotive is ready to move off shed when pressure is between 100 and 120 lbs/in^2, an hour or so after this.

June 1993

Tony Bennett cleans the paintwork around No 7's left hand cylinder.

September 1991

During the regular winter maintenance routine Pete Mintoft carefully files flat the seat of one of No 7's safety valves.

March 2005

Andy Young studies the fire he has lit in No 6 and decides where to put just one more piece of wood.

August 2003

Driver Terry Gurd looks the part in the cab of No 6 outside the shed in the morning sunshine.

June 2003

Terry Gurd adjusting one of No 6's left side valve gland nuts, prior to moving off to collect their train.

June 2003

Martin Fuller watering No 2 outside the shed. No 2 has its water tank at the rear of the cab and can be filled either from inside or outside the engine.

June 2003

No 2's driver side rear driving wheel and big end bearing.

March 2005

Martin Fuller adjusting the blower (left) and checking No 2's driver side injector (above) outside the shed. Steam locomotives require two independent methods of putting water into the boiler and both injectors are tested before the locomotive leaves the shed each morning.

June 2003

Nicky Fox cleaning ash from No 2's smokebox. She will also inspect the smokebox and boiler tubes for defects before carefully sealing the smokebox door ready for light-up

August 2003

Few photographers brave the dirt and occasional drips of hot water and oil to capture what goes on in the locomotive pit in the morning. However, there is reward for the intrepid as the cleanliness of Talyllyn engines' undersides can be admired. Here Pete Mintoft is cleaning No 1's motion.

August 2002

John Scott oiling No 6's driver side expansion link.
June 1999

Iolo Davies polishing No 1's driver side maker's plate.
July 1990

Roy Smith filling No 7's mechanical lubricator outside the shed.

June 1993

No 7's rear buffer beam. Talyllyn rolling stock is unusual on the narrow gauge in having side buffers. The pipe in the centre provides the air brake connection to the train.

June 2004

No 7's safety valves, steam dome and chimney.

June 2004

During 1990, film maker Graham Whistler visited the Talyllyn to record the railway for a commercial video of the line, simply called 'Talyllyn Railway', which was released the following year. Here he is filming No 1 being watered outside the shed by Graham Jenkins and Matthew Smith.

July 1990

Driver John Robinson applying oil to No 1's steam brake valve. This is lubricated each morning with cylinder oil containing graphite powder, which helps maintain easy movement of the valve throughout the day, even if the oil itself disperses.

September 2000

Mike Parrott gives the brass cover to No 2's driver side gauge glass a final polish.

August 1992

Tim Wroblewski applying Brasso to No 6's regulator lubricator. Having rubbed hard to remove the tarnish Tim will polish off with a soft cloth to give a good shine.

August 2003

Chris Parrott cleaning the eccentrics that drive No 1's valve motion.

June 2003

Dave Scotson setting a split pin on No 7's motion.

September 1991

Engineer Martin Turner replacing a rubber seal in the top fitting of one of No 3's gauge glasses. Over time these seals become brittle and eventually start to leak and require replacement.

August 2003

Tony Bennett gets a shine on one of No 1's brass nameplates. His reflection shows that he has already got a good finish on the paintwork.

June 2003

John Robinson tightening a valve spindle nut on No 6 after replacing the steam-tight packing that seals the joint around the spindle.

August 2003

Liz Green polishing one of the original features of No 2 - the brass handrail along the top of the boiler barrel.

September 2000

Julian Stow and Dave Scotson jacking up No 3 in the locomotive shed to replace a broken spring. The locomotive was ready for traffic again the next day.

June 1993

Driver Maurice Wilson on the footplate of No 7 in the yard at Pendre during its first year in service.

September 1991

Graham Thomas driving No 1 eases the stock out of the North Carriage Shed at the start of the day.

August 1997

In July 1999 No 2 was trial steamed without its cab and boiler cladding, following overhaul, for a visit from the boiler inspector. Here David Jones and Martin Fuller fill the tank with water prior to moving it into the yard.

July 1999

The unusual sight of No 2 without cab resting on the shed road.

July 1999

No 2's simple controls can be seen in this shot of the locomotive in the yard at Pendre without its cab.

July 1999

No 2 has finished its duties for the day and is resting over the ash pit. Driver Mike Green reaches for a clinker shovel to remove the fire. Liz Green, his wife, was fireman to him that day and watches from the water column.

September 2000

No 2's fireman's side gauge glass. This shows the level of water in the boiler and is one of the most important safety components of a steam locomotive. Allowing the water level to drop so that the top (or 'crown') of the firebox is exposed can lead to serious boiler damage.

May 2004

TAL-Y-LLY

Fireman Peter Kent Mason throws out No 2's fire into the ash wagon at the end of the day.

September 1991

Bill Heynes filling No 1's tank from Pendre water column.

June 1994

Fireman Tony Bennett likes a spotless engine and gives No 1's tank a final polish before the locomotive moves off to pick up its train.

June 2003

Chris Parrott doing the same job as the photo above, on the same locomotive nine years later.

June 2003

Steam locomotive boilers accumulate scale and sludge from the water that passes through them to create the steam. Regular 'blow downs' are carried out to remove these contaminants. A special valve in the firebox is opened and steam, water and impurities are discharged. Here No 2 enjoys a blow down in the shed. The challenge for the photographer is to take the photograph and then put the camera safely away before the cloud of warm water vapour reaches the end of the shed and saturates the equipment.

July 1992

Alex Eyres throwing out the remains of No 1's fire on a delightful summer evening, watched by Keith Foster and his son James.

July 2001

Sarah Foster is firing No 3 as it runs through Pendre with a down train. Alex Eyres watches from the footplate of No 1 on the shed road.

July 2001

One of the Talyllyn's longest-serving volunteers, John Slater, using the power hacksaw to cut bar for making fishplates in Pendre Works. John joined the Society in 1951 and visited the railway from his home in London most weekends until he died in July 2004. He wrote a newsletter after every visit. His last one was numbered 1778.

July 1992

Pendre Works

The Works at Pendre is sited behind the Locomotive Shed, on the south side of the line. It can carry out virtually all tasks required to keep the railway operating, including building and heavy overhaul of locomotives, construction of passenger and freight vehicles and maintenance of all the railway's equipment. The only jobs regularly carried out off-site are heavy boiler work and large metal casting. Pendre Works regularly undertakes work for other railways, and is also used by the local community for non-railway jobs that have need of the skills and facilities of the railway. This 'jobbing' work provides a useful additional source of income for the Talyllyn.

John Bate, another long-serving member of the Talyllyn community, attaching a spacer plate to No 4's pony truck in the works. John first travelled on the railway in 1947, joined the Society in 1951 and was appointed Chief Engineer in 1963. He retired in 1994 but still continues as an engineering consultant to the railway, a record of work now spanning over 50 years.

August 2003

Locomotive No 7, designed by John Bate, under construction in the works. Mike Green is finishing the hole in the rear buffer beam that will accommodate the draw hook.

August 1989

Engineer Mike Green trial fitting No 7's right hand piston valve. The steam dome cover is resting upside down between the water tanks and the chimney sits alongside on the works floor.

May 1990

No 3's frames in the works during a periodic overhaul. In the background John Slater is working on the milling machine.

September 1991

Heavy lifting tackle is stored neatly on the wall in the works.

June 2004

Engineer Mike Green demonstrating a light touch at the controls of the lathe as he makes a finishing cut to the tread of a wheelset.

August 1992

David Jones poses by No 1 in the works whilst Chris Price attends to a job between the frames.

August 1996

John Slater machining a fishplate on the milling machine.

August 2000

Gerald Cox tapping a thread in one of the castings that make up the Talyllyn's own design of air pump.

August 2000

Robert Frost inside No 7's firebox pauses for a smile whilst working on the engine's boiler tubes.

March 2005

Electrical and S&T Engineer Nick Smith in the Electrical Workshop at Pendre.

June 2004

Maria Wagland at work in the Joinery Shop at Pendre.

June 2004

Martin Turner draw filing the mating surface of an air brake casting in the works.

August 2003

John Slater using the 'Pug' gas cutter to cut fishplate blanks from a sheet of steel.

June 1994

Peter Fuller firing No 1 with a down train arriving at Pendre.

June 1994

Pendre station nameboard adorned with ivy.

June 2004

Flowers decorate most stations on the Talyllyn, and Pendre is no exception. These campanula grow happily on the slate wall at the west end of the platform.

June 2004

It is late afternoon and No 3, fired by Sarah Foster and guarded by Steve Mort, passes over the level crossing into Pendre with a train from Nant Gwernol. Sarah's brother James has opened the crossing gates for the train.

July 2001

When the weather is fine it is traditional for works staff and volunteers to drink their tea on the platform at Pendre. Those present here include Graham Jenkins, Dave Scotson, John McCanna, Gerald Cox, Mike Green, Tim Tincknell, Dave Clarke and Tim Wilkinson.

June 1993

PENDRE TO RHYDYRONEN

Jeff Shuttleworth driving No 3 with an up train crossing Ty Mawr.
The whistle board is for down trains approaching Pendre.

May 2005

Pete Mintoft driving No 1 on the crossing at
Pendre with an up evening train.

July 2001

Pendre to Rhydyronen

From Pendre, the train passes over the road crossing, usually manned by
volunteers from the shed, and starts its journey up the Fathew Valley.

Passing the new industrial estate on the north side, the train then travels
under Ty Mawr Bridge and immediately starts to climb Hendy Bank.
This begins with one of the steepest stretches on the line – a short section
of 1 in 69. Half way up the bank is Hendy Halt, which is used by those
staying at the adjacent farm.

At the top of Hendy bank, the train passes under Hendy Bridge and the
gradient eases towards the next halt at Fach Goch.

No 7 with a down train crosses Ty Mawr and whistles for Pendre.

September 1991

At Fach Goch there was a siding from 1971 to 1982, and even an intermediate block instrument, housed in a small cabinet beside a ground frame that controlled access to the siding. This was largely used for dumping spoil that arose from excavations in Wharf Cutting and to build the new West Carriage Shed at Pendre. It also usefully filled-in for the farmer a boggy patch on the south side of the line up against the railway embankment.

The area is now grassed over and there is no evidence of where the siding once was, with the exception of the fence, which remains on the siding's alignment to the south side of the line.

The next bank is Cynfal, which finishes soon after the line crosses over a small stream and under Cynfal road bridge. Just beyond is Cynfal Halt, used by walkers and also visitors staying at Cynfal Farm, which is visible on the south side of the line.

From Cynfal it is an easy run to Rhydyronen, the first station outside Tywyn, and the first intermediate station to be built on the railway.

Dave Scotson driving No 4 with a down train emerges from Cynfal bridge.

May 2005

A view up Cynfal Bank looking out of the rear of the Talyllyn's ex-Corris Railway carriage. Travelling with me is John Smallwood.

June 1995

Cynfal halt and the line towards Rhydyronen.

May 2005

RHYDYRONEN

Maurice Wilson driving No 7 arriving at Rhydyronen with an up morning service.
September 1991

Rhydyronen

This station has been kept as close to its 1860s state as possible, with its original station building and tree-lined surroundings. The grass is tended by local volunteer Tony Bennett and the whole area is a picture in the spring with a fine display of daffodils and other early flowers.

The main changes here in recent years have been the removal of the short siding that existed in pre-society days, together with the extension and re-alignment of the platform which this allowed. The station makes a picturesque backdrop for photography on a sunny day, and gets regular use from visitors staying at the adjacent camping and caravan site.

Graham Jenkins, firing No 3, chats to the guard, Nigel Adams, at Rhydyronen. The occasion was a special early morning photographic train, organised to take pictures for the next year's timetable.

June 1995

Roy Smith driving No 7 as it enters the station at Rhydyronen. The station building is brightly lit by the morning sun.

June 1993

Driver Maurice Wilson and fireman Ken Timpson keep their eyes on the photographer from No 6 as they wait to depart from Rhydyronen with an up train. Guard Andy Young observes from the platform.

August 1996

Driver Roy Smith arriving at Rhydyronen with an up train amongst the spring daffodils. Bob Morland is the fireman and his daughter Kay takes her own picture from a convenient vantage point. (Gillian Morland)

April 1996

Everyone who travels on the Talyllyn will know this remarkable sign at Rhydyronen which is gradually being devoured by the tree to which it is attached.

May 2004

Rhydyronen station at its best with a carpet of daffodils to welcome the spring passengers.

April 1996

John Robinson driving No 1 arriving at Rhydyronen with a springtime down train.

April 1996

One of Rhydyronen's benches with daffodils in the foreground.

March 2005

In the springtime primroses bloom in the garden bed beside the bridge at Rhydyronen.

March 2005

Fireman Keith Foster chats to guard John Smallwood whilst No 2 rests with its Vintage Train at Rhydyronen. The locomotive headboard is celebrating the first fifty years of the Talyllyn Railway Preservation Society, which was formed in 1951.

September 2001

Guard Brian Sampson gives the 'right away' to fireman Peter Kent Mason on No 2 with an afternoon down train at Rhydyronen.

September 1991

Steve Griffiths driving No 5 through Rhydyronen with an engineering train. Behind the locomotive is one of the railway's useful 'Boflat' wagons, so named because they were originally used at Bowaters Paper Mill. This Boflat is fitted with a small crane for lifting heavy materials on and off its load space.

September 1997

No 2 arrives at Rhydyronen on a sunny morning to pick up a group of passengers who are out for a day's walking in the hills.

September 1991

Driver Maurice Wilson, fireman Graham Jenkins and guard Nigel Adams waiting for a sign from the photographer that he is ready for them to depart from Rhydyronen with an early morning photographic special, hauled by No 3.

June 1995

John Burton driving No 7 arrives at Rhydyronen with an up train.

June 1993

Stationmaster Sue Palmer relaxes in the sunshine between trains at Rhydyronen. With its daffodils in spring and roses through the summer, Rhydyronen is one of the most picturesque stations on the Talyllyn.

May 2004

Stationmaster Sue Palmer supervises her son Christopher who is showing a yellow flag (it has a black back) from the platform to an approaching train. This indicates to the driver that the train should stop for passengers at Rhydyronen station. No 3 can be seen approaching under the bridge.

May 2004

No 2 piloting No 1 with a down train leaving Rhydyronen. Martin Fuller is firing No 2 and visiting Swanage Railway fireman Oliver Furnell is on No 1.

June 2003

Ray Reid driving No 3 with an up train arriving at Rhydyronen.

April 1996

Pete Mintoft driving No 3 arriving at Rhydyronen with an afternoon down train.

May 2004

Driver Graham Thomas on No 2 arriving at Rhydyronen with an up train.

September 2002

David Ratcliff brings No 4 and its train for Nant Gwernol into Rhydyronen.

August 1992

In autumn half term Rhydyronen station is transformed into 'Hogsmeade' and is the scene for a game of Quidditch. This is played by young volunteer 'Tracksiders' and their parents, who are working on the railway that week. Here David Jones driving No 3 pulls away from the temporarily renamed station with a late afternoon train.

October 2004

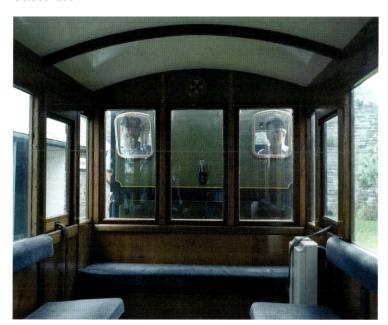

An unusual shot of the crew of No 7 at Rhydyronen, taken from inside the saloon carriage next to the engine. Just visible through the left spectacle plate is fireman Tony Bennett and on the right is driver Phil Guest.

September 1997

No 3, driven by David Jones, sets off into the late afternoon sun with the last train of the day back to Tywyn.

October 2004

Bill Heynes driving No 6 with an up train leaving Rhydyronen.

July 2001

Rhydyronen to Brynglas

Leaving Rhydyronen the train immediately passes under the road bridge and climbs a short sharp bank to cross a stream before easing to run past the Tynllwyn Caravan Park, where many railway volunteers stay during their visits to Tywyn. Trains often whistle to children watching at the gate, and then again for Tynllwyn Hen Halt, which is just around the next bend. The halt is sometimes used by walkers as it gives access to a track into the hills to the south.

The line then continues on a gentle climb through the pastures towards Brynglas, passing an occupation crossing for Brynerwest Farm, which is across the fields on the north side of the line. Brynglas is approached via a short ledge cut into a rock outcrop on the south side of the line.

John Robinson is firing No 1 as it leaves Rhydyronen and crosses the stream bridge just before passing Tynllwyn Caravan Park.
May 2003

Graham Thomas and No 2 leaving Rhydyronen with an up train. This can be a difficult start for a locomotive on a damp day with a heavy train. Today the sun is shining and the rails are dry so No 2 has no trouble lifting its train up the grade.

September 2002

No 2's driver side crosshead.

March 2005

A view along the railway up the valley towards the halt at Tynllwynhen. The trespassers sign is adjacent to a footpath that crosses the line here.

May 2004

Paul Shuttleworth driving No 7 with a down train across the stream bridge just above Rhydyronen.

May 2004

On a pleasant summer afternoon Sarah Foster is firing No 3 as it coasts round the bend into Rhydyronen with a train for Tywyn.
July 2001

Jeff Shuttleworth driving No 6 over the stream bridge above Rhydyronen with an up train,

June 2003

Detail of the clack valve on the fireman's side of No 6's boiler.

May 2004

The alert traveller will spot this toadstool, one of several carved from old tree stumps by volunteer Tony Bennett. It is on the south side of the line just above the Rhydyronen stream bridge.

May 2004

No 2 and No 3 double-heading a down train approaching Rhydyronen. Sarah Foster is firing No 2 and Ken Timpson No 3. Just visible also is Julian Stow driving No 3.

July 2001

The sky looks a little threatening but the sun is still out for this shot of the up whistle board for Tynllwynhen halt, which is just around the right hand bend ahead.

May 2004

No 3 with an up special train approaching the Tynllwyn farm crossing, crewed by Maurice Wilson and Graham Jenkins. The horses in the field beside the line have seen the train many times before and aren't that interested this morning.

June 1995

Tynllwynhen halt (left) and the track up into the hills to the south (right).

May 2004

Julian Stow driving No 1 with a summer morning train above Tynllwynhen.

August 2003

Driver John Robinson and fireman Ian Lloyd-Owen on No 6 coasting down between the hedgerows towards Tynllwynhen with an afternoon train from Nant Gwernol.

May 2004

Maurice Wilson driving No 3 through the trees above Rhydyronen.

June 1995

Gareth Jones on No 2 has just passed Tynllwynhen and the train is on its way towards Brynglas.

August 2003

Don Newing driving No 6 whistles on the approach to Brynglas. In the background the sea looks inviting, but Cardigan Bay is usually cold unless the weather has been hot for several days.

June 2004

Milepost two and a half is just above Tynllwynhen. The box beyond the milepost contains a telephone point. In an emergency, the guard may connect a portable telephone, kept in each brake van, and call Control at Wharf for assistance.

May 2004

Driver Colin Roobottom on No 6 coasting down from Brynglas. The hill across
the valley is Foel Wylett, which rises to a height of 1013 ft.

September 2002

No 4 with a photographic special whistles for Brynglas on a cool autumn morning. The photographers have got off the train and are in the field to the left. No 4 has made several run-pasts so they all get the opportunity to take a number of shots.

October 2004

Driver Pete Mintoft and fireman Rob Plumridge on No 7 with its train at Brynerwest, between Brynglas and Tynllwynhen. Just visible through the spectacle plate is Keith Alger, who is travelling 'third man' as part of his footplate training.

August 2003

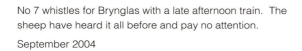

No 7 whistles for Brynglas with a late afternoon train. The sheep have heard it all before and pay no attention.

September 2004

Gareth Jones on No 1 leaving Brynglas with a down train. Brynglas blockpost can be seen just above the train.

September 2003

No 4 with a running-in special approaching Brynglas. At the back of the short train is No 9, to provide some weight and just in case they need help to get home (they didn't, of course).

May 2004

No 7 with an up train approaching Brynglas. In the background the Fathew valley runs down to the sea at Tywyn.

September 2002

BRYNGLAS

Bill Tyndall looks cheerfully from the cab of No 7 as it leaves the loop at Brynglas after crossing an up train.

July 2001

Brynglas

Trains may cross at Brynglas loop, and will stop here for the fireman to exchange tokens when no blockman is on duty to perform this job. There is also a siding here, used for stabling engineering trains.

After the loop the line crosses the lane leading to the hamlet of Pandy, and Brynglas station is immediately beyond. On the south side of the line at the station is the Memorial Garden, where the ashes of many who have loved the Talyllyn have been laid to rest, within earshot and just a few yards from the passing trains.

Brynglas station sign and instructions to passengers wishing to purchase tickets.

June 2004

No 3 rests at Brynglas with a late afternoon down train. The fireman, Phil Glazebrook, is entering the blockpost to exchange tokens.

September 2004

The Brynglas Flood

On 10th June 1993 there was heavy rainfall in the hills above Brynglas, and a huge quantity of water built up behind a dam made up from rubble and trees washed off the hillside. Suddenly this dam broke and a torrent swept down the valley, flooding the houses in the hamlet of Pandy and washing much of their furniture across the railway and down into the field below the loop.

Fortunately the last train of the day had just passed safely down when the flood occurred, but considerable damage was caused to the track, and trains had to be diverted through the loop whilst repairs were carried out. The retaining wall, now visible along the north side of the line, was rapidly designed and built, and there was much clearing up needed before trains could cross again at Brynglas.

On 12th June 1993, two days after the flood, work is well advanced on clearing up the mess and building a new retaining wall where the railway foundation had been washed into the field below.

Top left: A view up the valley showing the mass of rocks and debris that had come down. The machines are stabilising the banks and clearing up the mess in the gardens of the houses that make up the hamlet of Pandy.

Centre left: Filling behind the new retaining wall.

Bottom left: The gang watches as No 3 passes through the loop with an up train. Those pictured include John Bate, Graham Jenkins, Tim Tincknell, Darren Pegg, Dave Clarke, Jon Richmond, Eddie Castellan and Chris Parrott.

Below: An unofficial green flag is given as a tipper wagon full of spoil is shunted by Richard Evans, Richard Pickersgill and Chris Parrott.

Ian Dods, Jon Richmond and Graham Jenkins
(on No 8) discuss the next move required by the
team building the new retaining wall.

June 1993

Jon Richmond watches the gang at work
from inside the blockpost. A local cat
frequents the blockpost at Brynglas,
coming and going through a gap where
the point rodding exits the cabin. When
the flood had subsided enough to allow
inspection of the mess, the cat was found,
wet but unharmed, inside the blockpost.

June 1993

No 3, fired by Phil Glazebrook, leaving Brynglas with a down train. Sue Whitehouse is
the guard looking out of the van.

September 2004

Brynglas blockman Paul Lazell catches up on some reading in a quiet moment between trains.

June 2004

Telephone and Electric Key Token instrument for the section from Brynglas to Pendre. The switch on the yellow box behind the instrument engages a 'remote operator' function, allowing a token to be withdrawn at Pendre when Brynglas Blockpost is unmanned.

June 2004

Since the Brynglas flood in 1993, a lifebelt has been standard issue in the blockpost.

June 2004

At the end of the summer, haymaking is an important part of the year for the valley farmers. Here 'big bales' are being wrapped close to the farm crossing at Brynglas.

September 2004

During the summer holiday there is often a camp at Brynglas for visiting religious groups. Here their neat rows of tents can be seen in the field. The large tent is their mess.

August 1996

The warning sign at the farm crossing just above Brynglas station. In the background is the station building and beyond this the blockpost can just be seen.

June 2004

A mixed line-up in the siding at Brynglas. Closest to the camera is the frame of diesel No 9's twin, purchased for spares along with No 9 in 1970. Behind this is an assortment of iron body wagons and at the end is the tool van.

September 2004

No 3 rests in the station at Brynglas with a down train.

September 2004

No 3's number plate, and reminder that the locomotive spent the first 70 years of its long life on the neighbouring Corris railway. It has now been on the Talyllyn for over 50 years.

September 2004

Driver and Locomotive Inspector Phil Guest has time to draw on his pipe as No 3 rests at Brynglas with a down train. The fireman is in the blockpost obtaining the token that will allow them to proceed to Pendre. The guard, Sue Whitehouse, is waiting in the van with green flag ready to give the 'right away' when the fireman returns.

September 2004

These attractive purple linaria grow wild alongside the line at Brynglas.

September 2004

When the blockpost is manned, the blockman puts out 'Stop' boards. Trains must stop at the boards until called forward by a flag signal from the blockman. This is the Brynglas down stop board.

June 2004

Andrew Thomas poses on the footplate of No 4 in the loop at Brynglas on a photographic special.

October 2004

Many flowers adorn the hedgerows throughout the summer. These campions are on the bank of Tadpole Cutting, just above Brynglas.

September 2004

Much of the Talyllyn was originally fenced using irregular slabs of slate placed vertically with their tops linked by thick wire. A surprising amount of this slate fencing survives, some in original condition, especially in the woods between Abergynolwyn and Nant Gwernol. The railway conserves the remaining slate fencing and is also rebuilding fences in the traditional way, such as this one at Brynglas.

September 2004

Alongside the line at Brynglas is the Memorial Garden, which is home to the ashes of members who enjoyed working and travelling on the Talyllyn during their lifetimes.

March 2005

Blackberries provide a welcome snack for anyone working on the lineside in late summer. These ones are just above Brynglas.

September 2004

Foxgloves thrive on the lineside at Brynglas and make a colourful sight in early summer.

June 2004

Driver Simon Jenkins looking relaxed on the footplate of No 4 with a photographic special train at Brynglas. The train comprises three slate wagons, two iron body wagons and the Corris Van, with a carriage at the rear for the photographers. The Corris Van was supplied to the Corris Railway by Falcon Works, Loughborough, in 1885. A remarkable survivor, it has been extensively rebuilt but retains the same basic design as the original.

October 2004

Fireman Phil Glazebrook watches the station and crossing ahead as No 3 arrives at Brynglas with a down train.

September 2004

No 1, crewed by Dave Scotson and John Burton, running through Brynglas. Blockman Winston McCanna waits on the crossing to exchange tokens with the fireman. Meanwhile, driver Maurice Wilson waits by the blockpost to collect the token that will allow him to take his train, which is in the loop on the left, down to Pendre.

June 1995

Driver Simon Jenkins and fireman Andrew Thomas on No 4 as it gently runs over the crossing at Brynglas.
By the blockpost is the blockman, Helen Carlyle.

October 2004

No 4's maker's plate.

May 2004

Martin Turner firing No 4 at Brynglas crossing on a delightful evening in early summer. Pete
Mintoft had also travelled up to Brynglas to see the train pass, and watches from beside the
line. In the train for the ride are locomotive department volunteers Alex Eyres and Bill Heynes.

May 2004

Simon Jenkins and Andrew Thomas on No 4 with a photographic special at Brynglas.

October 2004

Driver Maurice Wilson with No 3 and an up train on the farm crossing above Brynglas.

June 1995

Brynglas to Dolgoch

Leaving Brynglas, the line crosses a track connecting the farm with fields on the north of the line and climbs through Tadpole Cutting – named by the early preservationists in the 1950s due to its tendency to flood to a depth of a foot or more in wet weather, thus providing a fertile habitat for numerous tadpoles. Half way up the cutting is Brynglas Bridge and soon after this the train emerges onto an embankment from which travellers can get their first real view up the valley towards Wales' second highest mountain – Cader Idris.

Climbing all the time we soon reach Six Bends and emerge onto Doldeheuwydd Bank, named after the farm on the opposite side of the valley. As the train reaches the top of the bank the view of the valley opens out again and we soon enter the woods that surround Dolgoch. Emerging from another rocky outcrop the line crosses Dolgoch Viaduct – the largest civil engineering structure on the railway – and then passes through another rock cutting and into Dolgoch Station.

David Jones driving No 3 with a down train passing the sleeper platform built in 2004 on Brynglas Bank as a base for rebuilding a cattle creep under the railway.

October 2004

Tracksiders and Navvies

'Tracksiders' is a unique programme allowing the youngest members of the Society to start enjoying voluntary work on the Talyllyn, which will be their railway to run in the future. Tracksiders meet regularly in Tywyn and carry out useful jobs on the railway, as well as having plenty of fun with barbecues, games of Quidditch and evenings on the beach.

A group of older young members, the 'Navvies', also put a lot of time into work on the railway. They are able to handle the heavier jobs that the Tracksiders cannot (yet) manage.

Talyllyn 'Tracksiders' and their parents having a break for lunch at a temporary platform on Brynglas Bank. This Tracksiders gang was working to clear undergrowth from around a cattle creep under the line, which was due to be rebuilt the following month during the railway's regular Outdoor Week. Pictured here are (left to right) foreman Ian Evans, Adam Kilgour, Julian Smith, Edward Farrar, Nicholas Smith, Daniel Smith and Zoe Morland.

October 2004

No 1 and its train silhouetted against the hillside above Brynglas.

June 1995

No 3 with an up train at Six Bends, between Brynglas and Dolgoch.

June 1995

One advantage with No 2 is that it has optional wooden seats which the crew can use on the down journey. Here driver Maurice Wilson demonstrates use of the driver's seat as the train crosses Dolgoch viaduct.

September 1988

The original Talyllyn Van No 5 has two sliding doors on the platform side. In good weather this allows the guard to travel in style whilst still keeping an eye on his train. Here John Smallwood is showing how it is done.

September 2001

Pete Mintoft driving No 1 whistles for the photographer with an up Vintage Train in the woods just below Dolgoch.

June 1999

No 7 poses for photographs with an up train on Dolgoch viaduct during its first season in service. The crew are Mike Davies and Tony Bennett.

September 1991

James Foster firing No 1 with an up train just about to enter Dolgoch woods. This was an evening departure during one of the Talyllyn's all-night steamings. Bill Heynes, travelling third man on the engine, has spotted the photographer and smiles from the cab.

July 2001

No 2 with an up train crossing the viaduct and about to pull into Dolgoch station. The driver is Viv Thorpe and the fireman is Bob Morland. This was the first photograph of the Talyllyn taken with our Bronica SQ camera. (Gillian Morland)

August 1988

Fireman Peter Kent Mason looks the part on No 7 as it crosses Dolgoch viaduct with an up train on a balmy afternoon in late summer.

September 1991

No 2 rests at Dolgoch with an afternoon down train. Keith Foster and David Ratcliff pose obligingly for the photographer.

September 2001

Dolgoch

There is always a pause at Dolgoch for up trains to take water. The station is in a beautiful position in the woods, with a superb view to the south up the mountainside where the sheep give a scale to the scenery.

The station here first appeared in the timetable in 1867 and its main use over the years has been to bring visitors up to see the waterfalls. The Dolgoch Ravine offers some enchanting walks, with the river always close by for company and the noise of the falls never far away.

No 1 arrives at Dolgoch with an up train., driven by Graham Thomas. On the platform watching the train arrive are Graham's daughters, Caroline and Katherine.

August 1997

No 4 driven by Colin Roobottom arrives at Dolgoch with an up train.

July 1990

Matthew Smith and Colin Roobottom watering No 4 at Dolgoch.

July 1990

John Burton filling No 1's tank at Dolgoch on a warm summer afternoon.

June 1995

A view from the new water tower as No 7 brings its train into the platform at Dolgoch. On the left is the original water tower, now restored and usable by locomotives when they are hauling short trains.

July 1992

Everyone who has visited Dolgoch will know the gate (above) that guards the station from straying sheep. It has a simple closing device (left), typical of the Talyllyn - an old brake shoe threaded on a cable providing the necessary weight to pull the gate shut.

September 2004

During the period when No 6 was turned to face down the valley, Andy Young is on the fireman's side of the engine as it enters Dolgoch with a down train.

June 1998

The crew of a photographic special enjoy the early morning sunshine in the station at Dolgoch. On the engine is driver Maurice Wilson. On the platform are Gareth Jones, John Smallwood and Nigel Adams.

June 1995

The path from the station down towards the Dolgoch Falls Hotel winds through the old woodland alongside one of the many streams that tumble down the valley sides.

September 2004

The main path that runs up the Dolgoch ravine catches the evening sun. In the background, the viaduct can just be seen between the trees.

September 2004

The gate to the station, on the left of this picture and on page 154, is still needed to keep out the sheep. Here a flock is moving up the track to the cattle creep under the railway and onto the pastures of Talyfan, to the south of the railway.

September 2004

Guard Tony Thorpe standing in the doorway of the brake van as the train leaves Dolgoch for Abergynolwyn.

May 1998

No 1 rests in the station at Dolgoch with a down train. Driver Roy Smith and his fireman Martin Wilding relax on the platform.

September 1988

The rhododendrons at Dolgoch come into flower in late spring.

May 2005

Pete Mintoft has a smile for the photographer as his fireman, Dale Coton, finishes watering No 1 at Dolgoch.

June 1999

Stationmaster Leslie Sharpe in the Dolgoch booking office.

September 2004

Passengers waiting at Dolgoch for the down train, which is just arriving, hauled by No 4.

June 1995

The view down the Fathew valley towards the sea from the hillside of Talyfan. No 1 can just be seen entering Dolgoch station, amongst the trees in the centre of the picture.

June 1990

Looking down on No 4 as it brings its train into Dolgoch.

July 1990

Guard Lizzi Whitehouse waits for departure time. No 4 is the engine on this down train.

June 1999

No 6, facing towards Tywyn, in the station at Dolgoch with a down train.
Fireman Andy Young kindly poses for the camera.

June 1998

The pathway at the bottom of Dolgoch ravine, where routes diverge. To the left is the path to the station whilst straight ahead the track leads up the ravine, under the viaduct and on to the falls.

September 2004

Driver Bill Heynes filling No 6's tank at Dolgoch. Normally the hose would reach the filler, but on this occasion the fireman, who was driving under instruction, stopped a little short. In spite of this, the water still went in, and it made a good picture.

July 2001

John Hillman is stationmaster at Dolgoch as No 1 enters with a down Vintage Train. The blackboard welcomes travellers to Dolgoch, in English and Welsh.

June 1999

Steve Griffiths driving No 9 with an engineering train passing Dolgoch. Behind the engine is the Matisa ballast tamping machine and in front is a 'Boflat' wagon.

August 1996

Driver Mike Green has just finished filling No 3's tank at Dolgoch.

June 1995

Just opposite the platform a small stream trickles under the track. In the past, station staff advertised 'stream cooled drinks' here, but worries about infections in the water mean that this Talyllyn service is sadly no longer available.

September 2004

The fern-lined cutting just to the east of Dolgoch station. It acts as drainage for a bog on the hillside behind, and has always been very wet. A new drain has recently been completed here to improve stability of the trackbed.

September 2004

Dave Scotson is driving No 4 as they wait in the sunshine at Dolgoch for departure time.

June 1995

Mike Green checks the water level in No 1's tank. His fireman, Bill Heynes, waits on the water column to turn off the tap.

June 1994

Just by the lower falls the footpaths have recently been improved and new information boards added. Straight ahead the path zig-zags up the hillside to the upper falls, whilst to the left is the route to the station.

June 2004

The woods around Dolgoch are a haven for bluebells in the spring. These ones are on the bank opposite the station platform.

May 2005

The evening sun illuminates the trees of the old woodland in Dolgoch ravine.

June 2004

The lower falls at Dolgoch, as photographed by many thousands of visitors
who have travelled up on the Talyllyn Railway to see them.

June 2004

The river at Dolgoch emerging from the ravine into the main valley.
June 2004

The river above the middle falls at Dolgoch flows through a delightful setting amongst moss and ferns.
June 2004

Pete Mintoft on No 1 departs from Dolgoch with a train for Tywyn.
June 1999

DOLGOCH TO QUARRY SIDING

Driver David Jones and fireman Ian Lloyd-Owen on No 2 approaching Quarry Siding with an up train. They have just received a flag signal from the blockman to pass the stop board, which is to the right of the engine.

August 2003

Dolgoch to Quarry Siding

After departure from Dolgoch the train rounds a bend and soon approaches the next passing loop at Quarry Siding. Just before the loop at Quarry the line crosses a farm track giving access to the pastures on the hillside above. Trains will halt here on request to pick up or set down passengers.

John Robinson is firing No 3 as it pulls away from Dolgoch in this springtime picture, before the trees have their leaves.

April 1996

A close-up of the Talyllyn track just above Dolgoch as it catches the evening sun.

September 2004

The forest floor above Dolgoch is a carpet of bluebells in springtime.

May 2005

Chris Parrott on No 6 leaving Dolgoch with a morning up train, catching the sunlight beneath the trees.

August 1996

No 2 piloting No 1 with an up train on the crossing at Quarry Siding. Paul Shuttleworth is driving No 2 and fireman Tony Bennett gets in the picture too.

June 2003

Plenty of smoke in this shot of No 2 piloting No 1 with an up train just below Quarry Siding. Martin Fuller is just visible firing No 2 and Paul Shuttleworth is driving No 1. They are about to restart their train after pausing for a signal from the blockman.

June 2003

Gareth Jones and Phil Higginson are the crew on No 3 as they approach Quarry Siding with a special service run for the Talyllyn Railway Preservation Society Annual General meeting. Just visible at the rear, banking the train, is No 2 driven by Bill Heynes.

September 2003

No 1 generates an atmospheric smoke and steam effect as it restarts its train after a stop below Quarry Siding. Driver David Jones and fireman Peter Kent Mason are in charge. Carol Curtis is also on the engine and peeps out from the driver's side window.

September 2003

QUARRY SIDING

No 3, driven by Maurice Wilson and fired by Graham Jenkins, runs over the crossing at Quarry Siding.
To the left is the loop which allows trains to cross here.

June 1995

Quarry Siding

As its name suggests, Quarry Siding is home to a quarry, used in years past to extract stone for ballast on the railway. Unfortunately, the mudstone from the quarry made poor ballast as it tended to inhibit rather than encourage drainage. It has not been used by the railway for many years, but the siding remains and is often in use as a refuge for engineering trains and even occasionally for steam locomotives during special train services. Quarry also has a loop and the blockpost is often manned as crossings of passenger trains occur here regularly. When there isn't a crossing the fireman will leave the engine to exchange tokens.

The crew of No 1, Paul Shuttleworth and Tony Bennett, keep an eye on the photographer as they wait at Quarry Siding to cross a down train. Meanwhile, the crew of No 2, John Robinson, Martin Fuller and Ian McDavid (a visiting driver from the Swanage Railway), make use of the time by giving No 2's paintwork a quick polish.

June 2003

Mike Davies observes from No 7 as Gareth Jones and his family board the train at Quarry Siding halt, watched by the guard Tony Thorpe.

September 1991

The unusual sight of No 2 in the siding at Quarry. The occasion was a special train service where No 2 was acting as pilot and banker on trains to and from Quarry. Bill Heynes provides the picture with some additional interest in a characteristic pose.

September 2003

Another shot of No 2 between the trees at Quarry Siding, this time attached to the Corris Van. Bill Heynes has got into the photograph once again.

September 2003

Another unusual sight at Quarry Siding during a special train service. No 2 has run light engine to the top end of the loop to reverse into the siding, allowing trains to pass. Bill Heynes and Andy Young reluctantly agree to pose for the photograph.

September 2003

Details inside No 2's cab - the steam pressure gauge and the tops of the original Salter safety valve spring covers, both of which are carefully polished each morning by the fireman.

May 2004

No 2 and No 1 preparing to leave Quarry Siding with an up train, having just passed No 6 hauling a down train, which can be seen exiting the loop on the left. Climbing aboard No 2 is visiting Swanage Railway driver Ian McDavid. Paul Shuttleworth is driving No 1.

June 2003

No 1 and No 2 double heading an up train through Quarry Siding.

September 1992

Driver Phil Guest on No 6 at Quarry Siding.

August 1996

No 2 and No 1 make an impressive sight as they depart from Quarry Siding after crossing a down train. Blockman Tony Thorpe is preparing to hand the token for the section to Abergynolwyn to No 1's fireman. When a train is double headed, the token is shown to the crew of the leading engine and carried on the rearmost engine. Ian McDavid is driving No 2 and Paul Shuttleworth is in charge of No 1.

June 2003

Phil Mason and Neil Jones look ahead from No 3 as it starts its journey from Quarry Siding towards Abergynolwyn.

August 2003

Quarry Siding to Abergynolwyn

The line leaves Quarry and continues to climb – now on a ledge above the valley floor. Views over the valley on the north side are fine, but the observant traveller will also look out and up on the south side where the steep mountainside is usually a colourful mixture of heather and gorse, with rocky outcrops and the occasional sheep precariously standing, apparently with little effort, on the almost sheer mountainside. Buzzards often wheel over the crags and occasionally swoop down over the trains and across the valley. Red Kites also live here but stay up over the peaks and are more difficult to see from the railway.

LIMIT OF
SHUNT

Keith Foster driving No 6 as it crosses the cattle creep just above Quarry Siding. The 'Limit of Shunt' board indicates the point that an engine may run to from Quarry Siding without being in possession of a token for the section to Abergynolwyn.

September 2003

Driver Phil Guest enjoys the sunshine as No 7 steams away from Quarry Siding towards Abergynolwyn.

July 1992

Pete Mintoft driving No 1 with a down train just out of the woods below Abergynolwyn.

August 2002

No 4 whistles for Abergynolwyn with an up train, viewed from above on the mountainside of Mynydd Pentre.

June 1993

No 5's left hand side nameplate.

May 2004

Steve Griffiths driving No 5 with an engineering train approaching Quarry Siding and preparing to give the token to the blockman. He is hauling a 'Boflat' and the Corris Van.

September 1997

David Ratcliff driving No 6 with an up train approaching Abergynolwyn.

September 2002

The line continues to climb in a series of long straights, the second of which crosses a small ravine and stream called Ceunant Coch. This drains the northern slopes of Mynydd Tan-y-coed and tumbles down the slopes of Mynydd Pentre before passing under the railway and flowing down to join the Afon Fathew in the valley below.

Before long the line enters trees again and the view up the valley closes in to the point where Abergynolwyn Station sits, completely surrounded by woodland, on a ledge cut into the hillside.

No 2 leaves the woods below Abergynolwyn with a down train.

August 1988

Pete Mintoft driving No 1 as the train makes its way down from Abergynolwyn towards Quarry Siding. August 2002

Maurice Wilson on No 3 passing Ceunant Coch with a photographic special train.

June 1995

Driver David Ratcliff in relaxed pose as No 6 coasts down the line below Abergynolwyn.

September 2002

The stream at Ceunant Coch tumbles down the mountainside of Mynydd Pentre to pass under the railway on its journey to join the Afon Fathew in the valley below.

June 1993

Maurice Wilson driving No 7 with an up train passing Ceunant Coch.

September 1991

Driver Roy Smith on No 1 below Abergynolwyn. In the foreground is a stretch of traditional slate fencing.

August 1988

No 4 with an up train below Abergynolwyn. This was a challenging shot to take as the photographer was sitting on a convenient tree branch that reached out across the line. Getting safely onto and off the branch with a medium format camera and lenses was an interesting exercise.

June 1995

Previous pages: No 2 and its train on its way to Abergynolwyn are put into scale by the mountainside of Mynydd Pentre and beyond Mynydd Tan-y-coed, which rises to 1613 ft. (Gillian Morland)

August 1988

Tony Bennett driving No 7 with an up train passing Ceunant Coch. The locomotive headboard commemorates the life of Diana, Princess of Wales, who travelled on the Talyllyn Railway with the Prince of Wales in November 1982.

September 1997

ABERGYNOLWYN

No 2 and No 1 leaving Abergynolwyn with a down train. The firemen on both engines are visiting volunteers from the Swanage Railway - Nick Lloyd on No 2 and Daniel Bennett on No 1.

June 2003

Abergynolwyn

The station here has perhaps been most changed of all those on the Talyllyn. Originally the terminus of the passenger railway, Abergynolwyn sported a very small slate-roofed building which was quite inadequate to cope with the needs of modern travellers. The current station building was constructed in two parts in 1968 and 1999, partly using slate recovered from the Abergynolwyn Village incline winding house that had to be removed when the line was extended to Nant Gwernol in 1976.

Here also is the Talyllyn's longest platform, with space for two trains and more, together with a loop and the railway's largest blockpost building, which sports a 15 lever frame controlling points and colour light signals for the station and its approaches. Abergynolwyn is also a starting point for many passengers and recent developments here include the railway-themed playground and picnic area which is very popular with families.

The kind of Talyllyn scene that we would all like to remember. No 1 rests in the afternoon sun with the last up train of the day. The crew and passengers are taking their tea break by the station building.

May 1998

Gareth Jones enjoying the afternoon sunshine on No 3 as it prepares to leave Abergynolwyn with a down train.

June 1995

A view of Abergynolwyn station that not many people see. Looking down from the slopes of Mynydd Pentre onto the station in the middle of the woodland. No 4 is in the platform with a down train. Beyond, on the other side of the valley, is Foel Caerberllan, 1233 ft.

June 1993

A close-up of Abergynolwyn station from above, as No 4 whistles to leave with a down train.

June 1993

At the end of a beautiful warm day, No 7 leaves Abergynolwyn with a down train.
Flo Thorpe is the guard and Peter Kent Mason the fireman.

September 1991

The Talyllyn's Young Members' Group is very active and contributes significant effort to the maintenance of the railway. Here they are gathered in the blockpost at Abergynolwyn with driver Jon Mann during an evening Training Train. In the picture are Ivan Westley, Helen Carlyle, Andrew Thomas, Keith Alger, Tim Wroblewski, David Martin, Paul Cottrell, Adrian Rickard, Tim Willers, Dickie Garvey, Issy Williams, Jason Atkins, David Williams, Matt Dawson, Phil Eaton, Liz Garvey, Pippa McCanna, Neil Jones, James Hunter, Katie Willers, Nicky Fox and Caroline Howard. Members of the group were taking it in turns to work the train in the dark as firemen and guards. As you can see, an enjoyable time was had by all.

August 2003

Every year the Talyllyn joins with the people of Tywyn to celebrate Victorian Week. Staff, volunteers and passengers enter into the spirit by dressing in Victorian costume. Here fireman Bob Morland admires the etiquette of passengers taking tea at Abergynolwyn. (Gillian Morland)

July 1992

Blockman Bill Bishop making an entry in his Train Register in the blockpost at Abergynolwyn. The blockman records all train movements and times in the register as part of the discipline of running a public railway. The occasion was evening working to serve a Jazz Night featuring live music at Abergynolwyn station.

July 2001

A photograph that would be tough to repeat. The occasion was one of the Talyllyn's regular 24 hour steamings. The shot is taken with an 8 second exposure from the rear carriage of the 04:07 departure from Abergynolwyn. The sky in the east is just brightening and about half way through the exposure the train started, with a slight jolt, which resulted in the recorded movement of the two red colour light signals and lights on the station.

July 2001

Outside the peak season, trains stop by the station building at Abergynolwyn on the down journey for tea. This allows passengers and crew to take their refreshments close to the locomotive and train. Here No 1 is resting with its train, including original Talyllyn Van No 5, whilst everyone enjoys their tea in the sunshine.

June 1995

Ian Evans, driving No 6, wonders whether the photographer will successfully stay put on the steep slope as the train leaves for Tywyn.

August 1989

A study of No 1 at the head of its train during the afternoon tea break at Abergynolwyn.

May 1998

Mike Davies on No 7 chats to a young enthusiast at Abergynolwyn.

September 1991

Caught in flight, one of the family of Chaffinches that do well from crumbs left by passengers at Abergynolwyn. (Gillian Morland)

April 1996

Demonstrating the operation of one of the Talyllyn's unusual booking office brake vans, guard Chris White sells tickets to young passengers.

June 1993

The Talyllyn has working relationships with a number of other steam railways, ranging from the Ffestiniog in Wales to the Puffing Billy in Australia. One slightly closer to home is the Swanage Railway, with which regular exchange visits occur. Here on a Swanage visit to the Talyllyn are the two sets of crews together at Abergynolwyn. From left to right are Paul Shuttleworth, Tony Bennett, Martin Fuller, Daniel Bennett, Ian McDavid, John Robinson, Oliver Furnell, Steve Barker and Nick Lloyd.

June 2003

Two of the Talyllyn's longest serving drivers with No 1 at Abergynolwyn - on the left Roy Smith and on the right Dai Jones.

July 1990

During his last season driving before his retirement, driver David Ratcliff poses on No 6 with Martin Fuller, his fireman that day.

September 2002

A young admirer seems more interested in the photographer while for his father No 1 is the centre of attention.

August 2003

Bob Morland firing No 2 as it departs from Abergynolwyn with a down train. (Gillian Morland)

August 1988

No 2, driven by John Robinson, and No 1, driven by Paul Shuttleworth, double-heading a down train entering Abergynolwyn.
June 2003

A collection of vehicles in the siding at Abergynolwyn, with the line to Nant Gwernol curving away in the foreground. Behind the Matisa ballast tamping machine are two filled coal wagons. During the rebuilding work at Wharf it was not possible to store coal there, so it was delivered early in the morning to Abergynolwyn instead. There it was loaded into a variety of wagons, which were then hauled down to Pendre for use as required.

September 2004

Demonstrating the shunting of a slate wagon by hand are David Ratcliff, Dave Scotson, Michael Howard and John Babbs.

September 1992

Passengers and crew taking tea at Abergynolwyn while No 3 rests in the platform.
Driver and fireman on this occasion are Mike Davies and Ray Reid.

June 1993

Guard Tony Thorpe checks the train from Van No 5 as No 1 starts away from Abergynolwyn.

May 1998

Driver Phil Guest and fireman Mike Parrott in typically cheerful mood with No 2 and down Vintage Train at Abergynolwyn. The locomotive headboard celebrates the Talyllyn winning the Scania Transport Trust Award in 1992.

August 1992

In 2002, to celebrate the opening by Lord Faulkner of the new children's playground at Abergynolwyn, the 'Tracksiders' put on a performance of 'The Railway Children'. Seen here (left to right) are Tom Batchelor, Rosalind Goldrich, Josh Green, Sam Lolley, Clare Evans, Becky Warren, Richard Warren, Peter Austin and Simon Goldrich. The cast is acknowledging the applause from an appreciative audience including (above) Lord Faulkner and 'Tracksiders' organiser Ian Evans.

June 2002

Tracksiders Zoe Morland and Edward Farrar making good use of the Abergynolwyn playground, during a break from their Tracksiding work.

October 2004

The classic scene from 'The Railway Children' where the children flag down the train using Bobby's red petticoat. The 'train' in this performance was innovatively formed by the Tracksiders holding onto a long rope.

June 2002

Pete Mintoft enjoying the afternoon sun as No 1 leaves Abergynolwyn
with a down train.

August 2002

A photograph that captures the essence of the Talyllyn. Guard Tony Edwards acts as photographer
for a family posed alongside No 6 at Abergynolwyn.

June 2003

ABERGYNOLWYN TO NANT GWERNOL

Maurice Wilson is driving and Christine Homer is firing No 2 a few minutes after leaving Abergynolwyn on the final section of its journey to Nant Gwernol.

August 1988

Abergynolwyn to Nant Gwernol

Now we are on to what used to be called the "mineral extension". The public railway originally terminated at Abergynolwyn, with the line beyond being used only for trains conveying slate from the bottom of the Alltwyllt Incline (the first of three giving access to the quarries at Bryneglwys) and by engines travelling up to Ty Dwr to take water. The extension of the passenger railway to Nant Gwernol was opened on 22nd May 1976.

The line now runs along the valley side and soon the view over Abergynolwyn village – considered by many to be the most appealing on the line – opens up to the north. One can also see, weather permitting, the peak of Cader Idris beyond Talyllyn Lake at the end of the valley. Soon the engine whistles for Forestry Crossing, the line's only crossing protected by lights.

Ian Lloyd-Owen driving No 1 as it rounds the bend to enter the station at Abergynolwyn with a down train.

August 2002

A view through the trees along the line towards Nant Gwernol. The old post in the centre of the shot dates from pre-society days and used to support a gate which could be closed across the line, probably to control straying livestock.

September 2004

The line from Abergynolwyn to Nant Gwernol runs through the forested slopes of Foel Fâch and Foel Fawr. Here No 2, driven by John Hague, emerges from the trees just above Abergynolwyn into a patch of sunlight before returning again to the wooded glade through which the railway makes its way at the top end of the line.

September 1988

No 1 with a down train crosses an embankment over a small stream just above Abergynolwyn.

May 1998

Eddie Castellan driving No 4 as it catches the sun with a down train approaching Abergynolwyn.

May 1998

Signal and telephone volunteer Richard Huss testing a lineside telephone just above Abergynolwyn.

May 1998

The view from the line up the valley to Abergynolwyn village and beyond towards Talyllyn lake.

September 2004

No 5 with a weedkilling train heads down through the woods towards Abergynolwyn.

June 1995

Tony Baker is firing No 7 as it hauls its train up towards Forestry Crossing.

September 2004

Maurice Wilson driving No 1 with an up train just after leaving Abergynolwyn for Nant Gwernol.
June 1995

All the trains were safely back in their sheds at Pendre when this shot was taken, on a beautiful late summer evening, when the sun just reaches over the hills on the north side of the valley to bathe parts of the line above Abergynolwyn in light. The blockpost is unmanned, hence the illuminated 'U' on the Abergynolwyn down home signal to the left.

September 2004

Abergynolwyn village basks in the evening sunshine.

September 2004

After the Forestry Crossing we plunge back into the woods and soon pass the waterfall and stream of Ty Dwr. Just beyond the stream, on the south side of the line, the observant traveller will see that a small level area has been cut out of the rock face. Here was built in 1865 the railway's original locomotive shed, where the line's first engine, No 1 'Talyllyn' was housed prior to the construction of the shed and works at Pendre.

In early society days it was still commonplace for engines to run light up to Ty Dwr to take water, utilising a simple wooden launder from which some water entered the tank but most poured over in a cascade onto the grass-covered track.

Chris Parrott with No 1 and an up train passing Ty Dwr.

June 2003

Maurice Wilson driving No 1 as it passes over Forestry Crossing with a train for Abergynolwyn and Tywyn.

June 1995

Another evening view down the line after the last train has passed. The whistle board and '5' sign on the left instruct drivers to slow to 5 mph and to whistle for Forestry Crossing, which can be seen in the centre of the picture. The car on the right belongs to the Talyllyn's Engineering Manager, who was also out enjoying the scenery at the top end of the line that day.

September 2004

No 2 guides its train through the woods above Ty Dwr, driven by John Hague.

August 1988

No 2 and No 1 taking the last left hand bend before the Abergynolwyn village incline winding house.

June 2003

Viv Thorpe with No 1 and a down train passing Ty Dwr.

May 1998

The picturesque waterfall at Ty Dwr.

September 2004

Close to the site of the winding house for the incline that once connected Abergynolwyn village to the railway there remains a well-built slate water tank.

September 2004

The line with Ty Dwr waterfall beyond. Left centre of the picture is the site of the original locomotive shed.

September 2004

John Burton driving No 1, rounds the last bend before arriving at Nant Gwernol station, and the end of the line.

June 1995

After Ty Dwr there are further glimpses of Abergynolwyn village through the trees and we soon round Big Bend and pass the site of the winding house for the incline to the village below. This was used for delivery of supplies to the quarrymen's cottages, and also for conveyance of 'night soil' away for disposal – somewhere on the railway. Turning towards the south, the railway now enters a narrow ravine off the main valley and soon reaches the end of the line at Nant Gwernol.

No 2 approaching Nant Gwernol with an up train at the end of its journey from Tywyn.

July 1990

John Burton driving No 1 crossing the loop points to enter the station at Nant Gwernol.

June 1995

A view down on Nant Gwernol from the slopes of Foel Pandy (1489 feet). No 2 is just arriving with an up train. Abergynolwyn village is in the valley beyond.

August 1988

No 1 departing from Nant Gwernol with a Vintage Train.

June 1999

NANT GWERNOL

Driver Mike Green and fireman Bill Heynes on No 1 crossing the loop points and entering Nant Gwernol. On the platform stationmaster Vic Thomas and a passenger watch the train coming in. Nant Gwernol is a challenging location for photography as the sun only comes over the high hills surrounding the station in the early morning and late evening.

June 1994

Nant Gwernol

The terminus station at Nant Gwernol was constructed completely new for the opening of the extension in 1976. It is on the site of sidings that were used for marshalling slate wagons travelling up and down the Alltwyllt Incline. The area needed considerable widening by blasting away the hillside to give the space needed for the new platform, loop and siding.

At Nant Gwernol travellers may watch the locomotive uncouple and run round its train for the journey back to

Tywyn. A simple ground frame, unlocked by a key on the single line Abergynolwyn to Nant Gwernol tickets, controls the points at the Tywyn end of the loop.

From the station there is a range of forest walks through the ravine, up the two inclines to the old quarries, back over the hillside and down the valley to Abergynolwyn. A gentler walk takes you along a path to the side of the Alltwyllt Incline, across a bridge and down the other side of the ravine.

A view from across the Nant Gwernol ravine of No 2 running round its train in the station.
The guard, Justin Adams, watches from the platform.

July 1990

No 2's maker's plate which proudly claims 'Fletcher's Petent'.
This refers to Dolgoch's unusual valve motion, which is driven
off the leading axle. When the Society took over the railway in
1950, the manager at the time, Edward Thomas, was reported
to have described this as 'a Very Peculiar Motion'. It is
certainly unconventional, but it has driven the engine up and
down the line for 140 years with very little trouble.

March 2005

It is usual for the driver to allow the fireman to run the engine round at Nant Gwernol. Here Nick Fieldhouse brings No 7 back into the platform to couple up to its train. Just visible on the fireman's side of the cab is the driver, Bill Heynes.

August 2002

No 3 rounds the bend into Nant Gwernol with the first train of the day.

June 1993

No 2 whistles for departure of its train. The Nant Gwernol stream is in the valley below.

July 1990

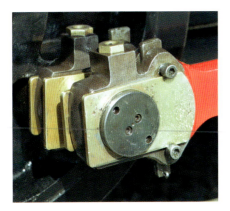

No 2's driver side big end bearing.

March 2005

The Nant Gwernol stream splashes over moss-covered rocks on its way down the ravine. The footbridge visible in the distance connects the station with a path that leads along the north side of the ravine and back down the valley to Abergynolwyn.

August 1989

Tony Bennett eases No 1 back towards its train after running round at Nant Gwernol. At the ground frame is engineer Dave Clarke, who is at Nant Gwernol carrying out maintenance work.

July 1992

The end of the line at Nant Gwernol. The point, with its hand lever to the right, allows locomotives to run round their trains on completion of their journey from Tywyn. To the left is a path that crosses the ravine and leads back to Abergynolwyn. Straight ahead the route is up the old Alltwyllt Incline towards the quarries.

May 2005

With the Alltwyllt Incline behind the photographer, this view shows the winding house, cut into a ledge in the rock face, and the points dividing the tracks for wagons travelling up and down the incline. The rod on the right of the picture operated the brake on the winding drum to control the movement of the wagons. The inclines worked by gravity alone, with the weight of the full wagons going down being used to haul the empty wagons up.

June 1998

The old rails at the top of the Alltwyllt Incline, the bottom of which is just behind the buffer stop in Nant Gwernol station. Loaded wagons from Bryneglwys Slate Quarries once descended this incline to be taken down the railway to Tywyn for shipment around the world, often by ship from Aberdovey.

June 1998

If the guard has an assistant he will often have time to help the locomotive run-round by operating the ground frame at the Abergynolwyn end of the loop. Here Mike Davies on No 3 receives the ticket, used to unlock the frame, from guard Peter Leppard.
June 1993

Conclusion

This then is the Talyllyn Railway. It is not the longest preserved railway, or the one with the most spectacular views. But it is the first railway in the world to be taken over and run on a voluntary basis by a preservation society. And it still runs under its original Act of Parliament of 1865, using both its original locomotives and all its original passenger rolling stock. This record is hard to beat.

For many of us who work on the Talyllyn, its life has become part of ours. The people we get to know here become our friends for life. If you know the Talyllyn and this book has brought you good memories of the Fathew Valley when the sun shines, then the project to produce it has been worthwhile. We have done even better if you have yet to seek out the railway hidden in its Welsh valley and these photographs encourage you to visit us to see the trains, enjoy the scenery and meet the people for yourself. You can be sure of a warm welcome and you will be joining with many generations of visitors from across the world who have come to travel on our trains and help us keep this special piece of Victorian engineering alive and well into the third millennium.

Guard Nigel Adams keeps a close eye on the train as No 1 leaves Nant Gwernol with its train back to Tywyn. Driver Maurice Wilson is on the fireman's side, allowing the fireman to drive the train under his supervision.

June 1995

Index

A

'a Very Peculiar Motion' 242
Abelson (Engineers) 21
Abelson, Douglas 21
Abergynolwyn 202
Abergynolwyn playground 218
Abergynolwyn village 226, 230, 239
Adams, Justin 242
Adams, Nigel 48, 87, 95, 156, 249
Admiralty Air Service Construction Corps 21, 51
Afon Dysynni 10
air brake 63
air brake casting 80
air brake hose 19
air pump 79
'Alf' 13
Alger, Keith 118, 206
all-night steamings 19, 147
Alltwyllt Incline 247
Andrew Barclay 21, 24
ash wagon 71
Atkins, Jason 206
Austin, Peter 218

B

Babbs, John 215
Baker, Tony 227
Barker, Steve 212
Batchelor, Tom 218
Bate, John 24, 40, 46, 76, 124
Bennett, Daniel 202, 212
Bennett, Tony 58, 66, 72, 86, 103, 109, 146, 174, 179, 201, 212, 246
Best, Andy 13, 15
big end 60
Bird Rock 10
Bishop, Bill 207
Blackberries 134
blow down 73
bluebells 168, 173
Bobby 218
'Bodgers' 31
'Boflat' 94, 164, 191
boiler tubes 79
booking office brake van 211

Bord na Mona 24
Bowaters Paper Mill 94
brake test 48
Brown, Malcolm 15, 43
Brown Marshalls 16
Bryce, Malcolm 36
'Bryneglwys' 40
Bryneglwys Slate Quarries 11, 247
Brynerwest 118
Brynglas Bank 142
Brynglas Blockpost 127
Brynglas down stop board 133
Brynglas Flood 124
Brynglas station sign 123
Brynhyfryd Road 20, 21
Burton, John 23, 26, 35, 96, 137, 152, 236, 238
Bwlch Llyn Bach 6, 254

C

'C' and 'T' boards 42
Cader Idris 254
campanula 81
campion 133
Cardigan Bay 10
Carlyle, Helen 56, 138, 206
Carriage No 12 32
Carriage No 18 30
Carriage No 22 30
Carriage No 4 29
Carriage Sheds 26
Castellan, Eddie 124, 225
Ceunant Coch 195, 196, 201
Chaffinch 211
'Chris Awdry Day' 19
clack valve 109
Clarke, Dave 82, 124, 246
clinker shovel 256
coal wagons 215
Corris Railway 14, 135
Corris Van 135, 181, 191
Coton, Dale 158
Cottrell, Paul 206
Cox, Gerald 79, 82
Craig Yr Aderyn 10
crosshead 106
Crowe, Walter 17
Curtis, Carol 177
Cynfal 85

No 4, fired by Martin Turner, leaves Brynglas with an evening train.

May 2004

D

daffodils 90
Davies, Iolo 62
Davies, Mike 18, 146, 180, 211, 216, 248
Dawson, Matt 206
'Deg' 40
Diana, Princess of Wales 201
displacement lubricators 45
displacement regulator lubricator 49
Dods, Ian 15, 48, 125
Dolgoch 150
'Dolgoch' 11
Dolgoch booking office 158
Dolgoch falls 169
Dolgoch ravine 161, 168
Dolgoch river 171
Dolgoch station 160
Dolgoch viaduct 145, 146, 149
Dolgoch woods 147
Dorman 40
'Douglas' 21
'Duncan' 21, 54

E

Eaton, Phil 206
ECS 16
'Edward Thomas' 14
Edwards, Tony 220
EKT 13
Electric Key Token 13

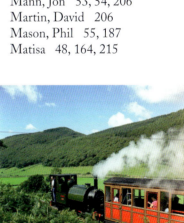

Pete Mintoft driving No 1 with a down
train below Abergynolwyn.

August 2002

Bill Heynes and Andy Young on No 2 at Quarry Siding.

September 2003

Passengers inspect No 1 and original Talyllyn Van No 5 at Nant Gwernol.

June 1999

Driver and Engineering Manager Dave Scotson walking back to the shed after a day on No 2. The observant will notice that he is carrying a broken clinker shovel, which will require a bit of welding in the workshop but will soon be back in service.

July 1992

Previous pages: A view of Talyllyn Lake, looking north east with the Bwlch Llyn Bach pass in the distance and the mountain of Cader Idris rising up on the left. The lake lies a further five miles up the valley beyond Abergynolwyn.

September 2003